Immigration to North America

Undocumented Immigrants and Homeland Security

Rick Schmerhorn

Immigration to North America

Undocumented Immigrants and Homeland Security

Rick Schmerhorn

Senior Consulting Editor Stuart Anderson
former Associate Commissioner for Policy and Planning,
US. Citizenship and Immigration Services

Introduction by Marian L. Smith, Historian,
U.S. Citizenship and Immigration Services

Introduction by Peter A. Hammerschmidt,
former First Secretary, Permanent Mission of Canada to the United Nations

MASON CREST
PHILADELPHIA

Mason Crest
450 Parkway Drive, Suite D
Broomall, PA 19008
www.masoncrest.com

©2017 by Mason Crest, an imprint of National Highlights, Inc.

Printed and bound in the United States of America.

CPSIA Compliance Information: Batch #INA2016.
For further information, contact Mason Crest at 1-866-MCP-Book.

First printing
1 3 5 7 9 8 6 4 2

Library of Congress Cataloging-in-Publication Data

on file at the Library of Congress
ISBN: 978-1-4222-3683-3 (hc)
ISBN: 978-1-4222-8100-0 (ebook)

Immigration to North America series ISBN: 978-1-4222-3679-6

Table of Contents

KEY ICONS TO LOOK FOR:

 Words to Understand: These words with their easy-to-understand definitions will increase the reader's understanding of the text, while building vocabulary skills.

 Sidebars: This boxed material within the main text allows readers to build knowledge, gain insights, explore possibilities, and broaden their perspectives by weaving together additional information to provide realistic and holistic perspectives.

 Research Projects: Readers are pointed toward areas of further inquiry connected to each chapter. Suggestions are provided for projects that encourage deeper research and analysis.

 Text-Dependent Questions: These questions send the reader back to the text for more careful attention to the evidence presented there.

 Series Glossary of Key Terms: This back-of-the book glossary contains terminology used throughout this series. Words found here increase the reader's ability to read and comprehend higher-level books and articles in this field.

The Changing Face of the United States

Marian L. Smith, Historian
U.S. Citizenship and Immigration Services

Americans commonly assume that immigration today is very different than immigration of the past. The immigrants themselves appear to be unlike immigrants of earlier eras. Their language, their dress, their food, and their ways seem strange. At times people fear too many of these new immigrants will destroy the America they know. But has anything really changed? Do new immigrants have any different effect on America than old immigrants a century ago? Is the American fear of too much immigration a new development? Do immigrants really change America more than America changes the immigrants? The very subject of immigration raises many questions.

In the United States, immigration is more than a chapter in a history book. It is a continuous thread that links the present moment to the first settlers on North American shores. From the first colonists' arrival until today, immigrants have been met by Americans who both welcomed and feared them. Immigrant contributions were always welcome—on the farm, in the fields, and in the factories. Welcoming the poor, the persecuted, and the "huddled masses" became an American principle. Beginning with the original Pilgrims' flight from religious persecution in the 1600s, through the Irish migration to escape starvation in the 1800s, to the relocation of Central Americans seeking refuge from civil wars in the 1980s and 1990s, the United States has considered itself a haven for the destitute and the oppressed.

But there was also concern that immigrants would not adopt American ways, habits, or language. Too many immigrants might overwhelm America. If so, the dream of the Founding Fathers for United States government and society would be destroyed. For this reason, throughout American history some have argued that limiting or ending immigration is our patriotic duty. Benjamin Franklin feared there were so many German immigrants in Pennsylvania the Colonial Legislature would begin speaking German. "Progressive" leaders of the early 1900s feared that immigrants who could not read and understand the English language were not only exploited by "big business," but also served as the foundation for "machine politics" that undermined the U.S. Constitution. This theme continues today, usually voiced by those who bear no malice toward immigrants but who want to preserve American ideals.

Have immigrants changed? In colonial days, when most colonists were of English descent, they considered Germans, Swiss, and French immigrants as different. They were not "one of us" because they spoke a different language. Generations later, Americans of German or French descent viewed Polish, Italian, and Russian immigrants as strange. They were not "like us" because they had a different religion, or because they did not come from a tradition of constitutional government. Recently, Americans of Polish or Italian descent have seen Nicaraguan, Pakistani, or Vietnamese immigrants as too different to be included. It has long been said of American immigration that the latest ones to arrive usually want to close the door behind them.

It is important to remember that fear of individual immigrant groups seldom lasted, and always lessened. Benjamin Franklin's anxiety over German immigrants disappeared after those immigrants' sons and daughters helped the nation gain independence in the Revolutionary War. The Irish of the mid-1800s were among the most hated immigrants, but today we all wear green on St. Patrick's Day. While a century ago it was feared that Italian and other Catholic immigrants would vote as directed by the Pope, today that controversy is only a vague memory. Unfortunately, some ethnic groups continue their efforts to earn acceptance. The African

Americans' struggle continues, and some Asian Americans, whose families have been in America for generations, are the victims of current anti-immigrant sentiment.

Time changes both immigrants and America. Each wave of new immigrants, with their strange language and habits, eventually grows old and passes away. Their American-born children speak English. The immigrants' grandchildren are completely American. The strange foods of their ancestors—spaghetti, baklava, hummus, or tofu—become common in any American restaurant or grocery store. Much of what the immigrants brought to these shores is lost, principally their language. And what is gained becomes as American as St. Patrick's Day, Hanukkah, or Cinco de Mayo, and we forget that it was once something foreign.

Recent immigrants are all around us. They come from every corner of the earth to join in the American Dream. They will continue to help make the American Dream a reality, just as all the immigrants who came before them have done.

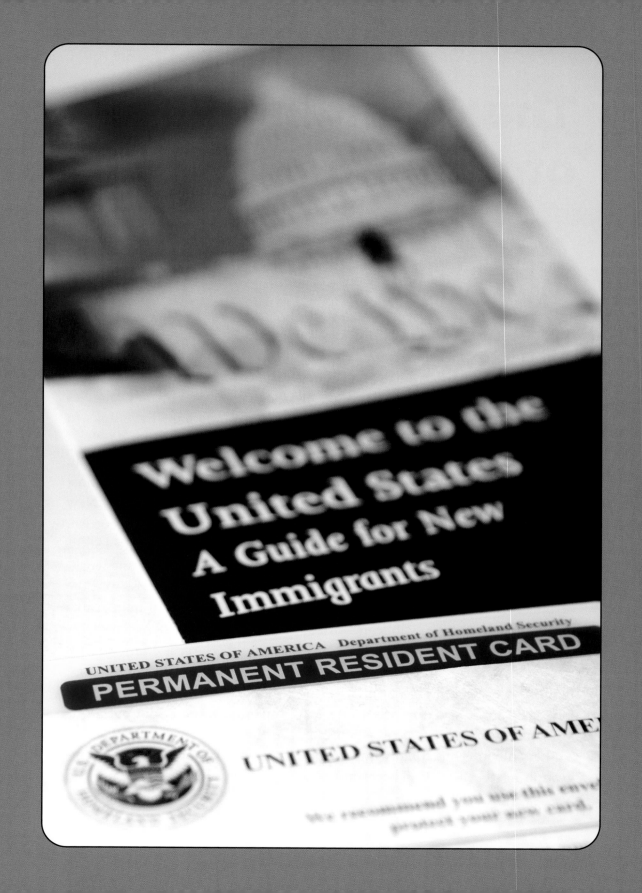

The Changing Face of Canada

Peter A. Hammerschmidt
former First Secretary, Permanent Mission of Canada to the United Nations

Throughout Canada's history, immigration has shaped and defined the very character of Canadian society. The migration of peoples from every part of the world into Canada has profoundly changed the way we look, speak, eat, and live. Through close and distant relatives who left their lands in search of a better life, all Canadians have links to immigrant pasts. We are a nation built by and of immigrants.

Two parallel forces have shaped the history of Canadian immigration. The enormous diversity of Canada's immigrant population is the most obvious. In the beginning came the enterprising settlers of the "New World," the French and English colonists. Soon after came the Scottish, Irish, and Northern and Central European farmers of the 1700s and 1800s. As the country expanded westward during the mid-1800s, migrant workers began arriving from China, Japan, and other Asian countries. And the turbulent twentieth century brought an even greater variety of immigrants to Canada, from the Caribbean, Africa, India, and Southeast Asia.

So while English- and French-Canadians are the largest ethnic groups in the country today, neither group alone represents a majority of the population. A large and vibrant multicultural mix makes up the rest, particularly in Canada's major cities. Toronto, Vancouver, and Montreal alone are home to people from over 200 ethnic groups!

Less obvious but equally important in the evolution of Canadian immigration has been hope. The promise of a better life lured Europeans and

Americans seeking cheap (sometimes even free) farmland. Thousands of Scots and Irish arrived to escape grinding poverty and starvation. Others came for freedom, to escape religious and political persecution. Canada has long been a haven to the world's dispossessed and disenfranchised—Dutch and German farmers cast out for their religious beliefs, black slaves fleeing the United States, and political refugees of despotic regimes in Europe, Africa, Asia, and South America.

The two forces of diversity and hope, so central to Canada's past, also shaped the modern era of Canadian immigration. Following the Second World War, Canada drew heavily on these influences to forge trailblazing immigration initiatives.

The catalyst for change was the adoption of the Canadian Bill of Rights in 1960. Recognizing its growing diversity and Canadians' changing attitudes towards racism, the government passed a federal statute barring discrimination on the grounds of race, national origin, color, religion, or sex. Effectively rejecting the discriminatory elements in Canadian immigration policy, the Bill of Rights forced the introduction of a new policy in 1962. The focus of immigration abruptly switched from national origin to the individual's potential contribution to Canadian society. The door to Canada was now open to every corner of the world.

Welcoming those seeking new hopes in a new land has also been a feature of Canadian immigration in the modern era. The focus on economic immigration has increased along with Canada's steadily growing economy, but political immigration has also been encouraged. Since 1945, Canada has admitted tens of thousands of displaced persons, including Jewish Holocaust survivors, victims of Soviet crackdowns in Hungary and Czechoslovakia, and refugees from political upheaval in Uganda, Chile, and Vietnam.

Prior to 1978, however, these political refugees were admitted as an exception to normal immigration procedures. That year, Canada revamped its refugee policy with a new Immigration Act that explicitly affirmed Canada's commitment to the resettlement of refugees from oppression. Today, the admission of refugees remains a central part of

Canadian immigration law and regulations.

Amendments to economic and political immigration policy have continued, refining further the bold steps taken during the modern era. Together, these initiatives have turned Canada into one of the world's few truly multicultural states.

Unlike the process of assimilation into a "melting pot" of cultures, immigrants to Canada are more likely to retain their cultural identity, beliefs, and practices. This is the source of some of Canada's greatest strengths as a society. And as a truly multicultural nation, diversity is not seen as a threat to Canadian identity. Quite the contrary—diversity is Canadian identity.

1 UNDOCUMENTED IMMIGRANTS

The second time the gang demanded money, José Miguel Cáceres realized he'd always be a target. José wasn't rich, but he did have a job. And, in his native country of Guatemala, that was enough to mark him for extortion.

José's troubles had begun one day during his shift at the McDonald's restaurant where he worked. Members of a local street gang were at the McDonald's, and they informed José that they'd like some money from him. José didn't need any further explanation.

Violent gangs control large swaths of Guatemala. Extortion, along with drug trafficking, is one of the main ways they make money. Guatemalans who resist paying gangs the money they demand face a brutal death. In general, reporting extortion threats to the authorities is unwise: Guatemala's police and military have proved unable to control the country's gangs—and in some places, according to various sources, corrupt authorities are actually in league with gangs.

José Miguel Cáceres decided he had no choice but to comply with the extortion demands. He scraped together the equivalent of about $400—a considerable sum in Guatemala—and paid off the gang members.

◀ Every year thousands of migrants illegally enter the United States by walking across the border or passing undetected through ports of entry. Many who make it into the country are deported after immigration agencies track them down.

Before too long, however, they visited José again. They demanded more money. When José stalled, gang members found out where he lived and began appearing at his house. They also phoned him repeatedly. They spelled out his options. "They told me they wanted money," the 20-year-old recalled to an American journalist, "and if I didn't give it, they were going to kill me."

José phoned his parents, who were living in Arlington, Virginia. They told their son he needed to get out of Guatemala as soon as possible. It was decided that José would join the rest of the family in Virginia. José's parents sent him some money to pay for his travel costs.

José's trip wouldn't be as simple as boarding a jetliner in Guatemala City and landing at Ronald Reagan Washington National Airport seven and a half hours later. To travel to the United States in that manner, he'd first have to get a Guatemalan passport. Then he'd have to fill out an application for a U.S. tourist visa and schedule an appointment at the U.S. Embassy in order to have the visa approved. The process could take weeks, and for José, waiting that long might prove fatal.

Instead, in early 2015 the young Guatemalan set off on a journey that, he hoped, would take him into the United States without proper authorization. If all went as planned, José Miguel Cáceres would join an estimated 11.3 million foreigners in the United States illegally. These people are known as "undocumented immigrants," "unauthorized immigrants," or, in some quarters, "illegal aliens."

Words to Understand in This Chapter

coyote—a slang term for those who smuggle undocumented immigrants across the Mexican border.

extortion—the crime of getting something, particularly money, through threats or the use of force.

national—a citizen of a particular nation.

A tattooed gang leader is arrested by police in El Salvador. Many undocumented immigrants come to the United States because they want to escape crime and violence in their home countries.

A Perilous Journey

Since the late 1970s, well over a million undocumented immigrants from Central America have entered the United States. A large wave came during the 1980s, when the region was beset by brutal civil wars. That wave petered out in the early 1990s, with the end of the civil wars. Around 2011 another wave began. It consisted largely of people fleeing violence related to drug trafficking and gang activity in Guatemala, El Salvador, and Honduras. A startling number of the migrants were unaccompanied minors, most of them teens but some as young as five.

The journey from Central America to the southern border of the United States, particularly for children and women, is fraught with peril. During the long trip through Mexico, many

A Mexican man wades through the sewage-filled New River to cross the border into Calexico, California.

migrants are attacked or robbed. Others are kidnapped by criminal gangs, who contact the migrants' relatives in Central America or the United States to demand ransom. In some places, corrupt Mexican officials also abuse and exploit migrants.

To traverse the roughly 2,000 miles (3,200 kilometers) from northern Guatemala to the U.S. border with Mexico, many Central American undocumented immigrants ride a network of freight trains known infamously as El tren de la muerte ("the Train of Death"). Thousands have lost their lives attempting to board, or falling from atop, moving boxcars or fuel tankers. Murders by bandits and gang members are common. Untold numbers of migrants have suffered violent assaults along the route.

Those fortunate enough to avoid being victimized by common criminals and organized gangs—and to elude arrest and deportation by Mexican immigration authorities—are by no means home free when they reach the U.S.-Mexico border. The United States has devoted considerable resources to stopping undocumented immigrants from slipping across the border. The effort begins with nearly 18,000 Border Patrol agents. They're aided by an array of high-tech equipment—from motion sensors and infrared cameras to drones—in addition to strategically placed fences and vehicle barriers.

To increase their chances of success, some undocumented immigrants pay smugglers to guide them across the border. These smugglers, known informally as "coyotes," may charge up to $3,000 per person, according to recent studies.

Across the Rio Grande

Most illegal immigrants attempt to cross the long border between the United States and Mexico.

José Miguel Cáceres joined five other Central Americans—two fellow Guatemalans, two Salvadorans, and a Nicaraguan—in hiring coyotes to guide them on the final leg of their journey to the United States. The group was taken to a safe house in Camargo, which is situated along the Rio Grande in the northern Mexican state of Tamaulipas. Across the river from

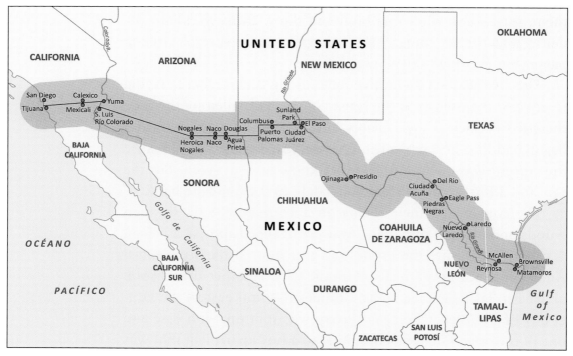

American Borders

The U.S.-Canada border is one of the longest in the world. It spans nearly 4,000 miles (6,437 kilometers)—not including the border between Alaska and Canada, which runs an additional 1,530 miles (2,462 km). In the south, the United States and Mexico share a border of more than 1,950 miles (3,138 km). Along these borders, there are over 300 land-based ports of entry. Separate from the borders are 12,383 miles (213,050 km) of coastline, as well as commercial airports through which people enter the United States. Considering these great dimensions, it's easy to see how large and complicated the task of controlling immigration is.

Camargo lies Rio Grande City, Texas.

Late one afternoon, after their clients had been at the safe house for several days, the coyotes decided the time was right to attempt a crossing. They loaded the six Central Americans into the covered back of a pickup truck and drove about five minutes to the banks of the Rio Grande. Almost immediately after emerging from the back of the pickup truck, however, the migrants were spotted by a U.S. Border Patrol helicopter. The men, along with the two Mexican coyotes who were to guide them, sprinted down a small hill and threw themselves into the dense underbrush there. The helicopter made several circling passes but eventually flew away.

The men walked about five miles along the riverbank, trying to conceal themselves in the brush. Night had fallen by the time the coyotes packed their clients into a small inflatable raft and began paddling across the Rio Grande. José was nervous because the current was swift and he didn't know how to swim. But the raft and all its occupants made it safely to the opposite bank.

The coyotes led their clients on a 15-minute walk through woods and along a dirt road. At a prearranged spot, a driver in a pickup truck met the group and transported the six Central Americans to a house in Rio Grande City. Another driver soon arrived to take the men some 40 miles (64 km) east to the larger city of McAllen. There, the group was split up, with José and one of the other Guatemalans going to a tiny apartment that was already occupied by an undocumented Honduran immigrant who'd been smuggled into the country months earlier.

The smugglers were to take their clients to Houston, but they needed to wait for bad weather, when there would be fewer Border Patrol checkpoints on the way north. After José had spent five days in McAllen, suitable weather came. The smugglers loaded José and 10 other illegal immigrants into the back of a large truck for the 350-mile (563-km) trip to Houston. But the truck never arrived at its destination. Border Patrol agents stopped and searched the vehicle, and José and the others were taken into custody.

José applied for asylum, claiming his life would be in danger if the United States sent him back to Guatemala. While his case was pending, he was placed in a detention center in Louisiana.

Border agents, particularly those employed in the Southwest states of Texas, Arizona, New Mexico, and California, routinely deal with illegal crossing attempts.

Who Are the Undocumented?

In 2012, according to estimates by the Pew Research Center, more than two-thirds of all foreigners in the United States illegally were Mexicans (52.4 percent) or Central Americans (15.2 percent). That perhaps shouldn't be too surprising, given the long land border between the United States and its southern neighbor, as well as the high levels of poverty and violence in Mexico and Central America. For many who slip across the U.S.-Mexico border, the United States offers hope for a more prosperous and safer future.

Of course, every undocumented immigrant has a unique story. And in order to understand the issues involved, it's essential to avoid overgeneralization. Statistically, the "typical" undocumented immigrant is a Spanish-speaker from the southern part of continental North America, but people from all cor-

A U.S. Customs inspector checks a woman's identity papers at the Paso del Norte port of entry in El Paso, Texas. After briefly asking a few important questions, inspectors will let most aliens through, although under special circumstances they may deny aliens entry.

ners of the world live in the United States without proper authorization. They come for a variety of reasons, and many arrive legally. Take, for example, a Chinese national who enters the United States on an F-1 student visa but decides to stay after obtaining her degree because she likes the freer social and political atmosphere in the United States. She is among the undocumented. So, too, is the Canadian who overstays his B-2 tourist visa to be close to the American girlfriend he met while vacationing in the United States. It's estimated, in fact, that 40 percent of the foreign nationals in the United States illegally first entered the country with valid documents but remained after their visas had expired.

Some "visa overstayers" remain for just weeks or months past their legally authorized time. On the other hand, many undocumented immigrants plan to spend the rest of their lives in the United States. In 2013, according to estimates by the Pew Research Center, the median period adult unauthorized immi-

U.S. President Barack Obama and Vice President Joe Biden meet with young undocumented immigrants whose deportation was deferred thanks to an Obama administration prgram, May 21, 2013.

grants had been in the country was close to 13 years. (In other words, half had been in the country for more than 13 years, and half had been in the country for less than 13 years.)

The long-term presence of undocumented immigrants has created a variety of complicated family situations. For example, persons in the United States illegally don't automatically qualify for U.S. citizenship, or even permanent resident status, if they marry a U.S. citizen. Hundreds of thousands of American citizens have an undocumented spouse who could be deported. And because any baby born on U.S. soil automatically acquires American citizenship, millions of U.S.-citizen children live with parents who have no legal right to be in the United States. In November 2014, President Barack Obama announced an executive action—known as Deferred Action for Parents of Americans, or DAPA—that would shield many parents of U.S. citizens from deportation (and grant them authorization to work in the United States). But a group of states led by Texas quickly filed a lawsuit challenging DAPA, and a federal judge issued an order blocking the program from being implemented. In April 2016, the United States Supreme Court heard arguments in the case; the Court was expected to issue a ruling by June.

The Immigration Reform and Control Act

Immigration in general, and illegal immigration in particular, proved a contentious political issue during the presidency of Barack Obama (2009–2017). But that was hardly unique in American history. The question of what to do about the nation's undocumented population had been arousing intense passions for decades.

By 1980, more than 2 million undocumented immigrants were in the United States, and in the years that followed, an estimated 200,000 arrived annually. In 1986, after several previous attempts had faltered, Congress finally passed legislation to address illegal immigration. President Ronald Reagan signed it into law on November 6, 1986.

The Immigration Reform and Control Act (IRCA) sought to

make illegally entering the United States more difficult and remaining in the country riskier. It did this by substantially increasing the number of Border Patrol agents and by imposing criminal penalties on illegal immigrants who used fraudulent

Asian migrants are discovered by U.S. Coast Guardsmen in the cargo hold of a ship in the Northern Hawaiian Islands. Stowing away in the cramped space of a ship is a typical—though often dangerous— method of illegal migration.

identity documents. The law also tried to remove the economic incentives for illegal immigration. Employers who knowingly hired undocumented immigrants faced fines or, in some cases, criminal charges—which, it was expected, would greatly diminish illegal immigrants' chances of finding work. The combination of stepped-up immigration enforcement and employer sanctions, IRCA supporters believed, would effectively stop the flow of illegal immigrants.

But what about undocumented immigrants who were already in the country? IRCA offered those who had been in the United States continuously since January 1, 1982, the opportunity to apply for legal status and, eventually, U.S. citizenship. Because the other provisions of IRCA were expected to prevent illegal immigration going forward, legalization was viewed as a one-time adjustment that would definitely put the issue to rest. But it was also seen in humanitarian terms. "The legalization provi-

A Hispanic family walks down the street of an immigrant neighborhood of Los Angeles. Because undocumented immigrants typically aim to blend into the legal migrant community, government agencies face a great challenge in locating and deporting them.

sions in this act will go far to improve the lives of a class of individuals who now must hide in the shadows, without access to many of the benefits of a free and open society," President Reagan noted in signing IRCA. "Very soon many of these men and women will be able to step into the sunlight and, ultimately, if they choose, they may become Americans."

About 2.9 million undocumented immigrants took advantage of IRCA's legalization provisions, leading to a substantial drop in the total number of people in the country illegally. But optimism that the law had solved the problem of unauthorized immigration soon disappeared. By 1989 the undocumented population had begun rising again—and it would increase steadily over the ensuing two decades, eventually peaking at more than 12 million.

Several factors explain the failure of IRCA to stop illegal immigration. First, even a 50 percent increase in the number of Border Patrol agents proved insufficient to secure the long border with Mexico. Moreover, sanctions against employers who hired undocumented immigrants weren't enforced fully or consistently. And the law required only that employers make a good-faith effort to check workers' documents; it didn't hold them responsible for failing to detect forgeries or falsified information provided by workers. That standard made it difficult to bring charges. Under the circumstances, many unscrupulous employers were willing to risk hiring illegal immigrants because they could pay those workers less, and make them work under more difficult conditions, than American workers would accept. Thus, IRCA did little to remove the economic incentives for illegal immigration, as the undocumented continued to be able to find work. Finally, while the legislators who drafted IRCA made it clear that the legalization of unauthorized immigrants already in the country would be a onetime occurrence, foreigners contemplating entering the country illegally didn't necessarily believe that. Many assumed that the United States would offer "amnesty" for unauthorized immigrants again at some point in the future.

Backlash

During the 1990s, as the number of undocumented immigrants in the United States grew steadily—from an estimated 3.5 million in 1990, to an estimated 5.7 million in 1995, to about 7.9 million in 1999—a rising chorus of anti-immigrant sentiment was heard. Critics blamed undocumented immigrants for a variety of problems. They said the undocumented took jobs from American workers, in addition to suppressing wages for Americans in certain low-skill occupations. Many critics complained about the costs of providing public services to unauthorized immigrants. They said that American taxpayers shouldn't have to bear those costs.

In 1994, voters in California—the state with the largest undocumented population—approved Proposition 187. Also known as the Save Our State initiative, Proposition 187 banned unauthorized immigrants from accessing services such as public education and health care (except in emergencies). Civil rights groups challenged the legality of Prop 187, and most of its provisions were eventually ruled unconstitutional in federal court.

Those who called for the government to crack down on illegal immigration didn't view the issue in economic terms alone. Many blamed undocumented immigrants for social problems such as high crime rates (though there's no evidence that undocumented immigrants are more inclined to criminality than the native-born population, and some studies suggest they actually commit less crime). Immigration critics also decried the cultural impact they believed the undocumented were having on the country. For example, much was made of the fact that the majority of illegal immigrants were Spanish-speakers, and that many of them knew little or no English when they arrived in the United States. Critics insisted that Mexican and Central American migrants weren't interested in learning English—a highly questionable assertion—and that this jeopardized the cultural unity of the United States. One anti-immigration group warned of a divided "America of hostile and competing ethnic groups."

Today, as was the case in the 1990s, the economic, social,

and cultural consequences of illegal immigration remain hotly contested. But another dimension of the issue has also gained prominence. What consequences could illegal immigration have for the nation's security? Might some people try to exploit the gaps in U.S. immigration enforcement not to seek economic opportunity or to escape danger in their home country but because they actively plan to do the United States harm? These questions assumed particular relevance in the wake of a shocking terrorist attack carried out in September 2001.

 **Text-Dependent Questions**

1. What factors were responsible for rising levels of Central American undocumented immigration beginning around 2011?
2. What was Proposition 187?
3. Name the 1986 law that supporters hoped would to solve the problem of illegal immigration.

Research Project

"Enrique's Journey," a six-part series by *Los Angeles Times* reporter Sonia Nazario, chronicled the odyssey of a Honduran teenager attempting to reach the United States. Read at least one part of the series at:
  http://www.latimes.com/nation/immigration/la-fg-enriques-journey-sg-storygallery.html
Then write a one-page summary.

2 THE SEPTEMBER 11 ATTACKS

In December 1979, troops from the Union of Soviet Socialist Republics (USSR) poured across their country's southern border with Afghanistan. The USSR, also called the Soviet Union, was a communist state. In invading Afghanistan, Soviet leaders wished to prop up a communist government there.

Afghanistan wasn't fertile ground for communism. Communists generally deny the existence of God, but the people of Afghanistan are deeply religious. Almost all of them are Muslims, or followers of Islam.

The Islamic faith originated on the Arabian Peninsula, in present-day Saudi Arabia, during the 600s. The religion spread quickly in the decades after the death of Muhammad, Islam's founding prophet, in 632. Today it's estimated that nearly one-quarter of the world's people are Muslims.

Followers of Islam are obligated to defend their faith, and fellow Muslims, against aggression. The Soviet invasion of Afghanistan thus triggered intense resistance among Afghans motivated not just by patriotism but also by religion. Using their country's rugged terrain to their advantage, Afghan fighters

◀ Smoke rises from the World Trade Center moments after two hijacked planes have crashed into its towers, September 11, 2001. As part of the investigation of the terrorist attacks, the Justice Department arrested and detained more than 1,000 undocumented immigrants.

known as *mujahideen* ("holy warriors") fiercely and relentlessly battled Soviet forces.

Muslims from around the world traveled to Afghanistan to join the mujahideen. And the governments of other Islamic nations, particularly Saudi Arabia and Pakistan, provided aid for the Afghan cause.

So, too, did the United States. The United States and the Soviet Union were locked in a long struggle for global influence known as the Cold War. (Most historians say the Cold War began in 1947 and lasted until 1991, when the USSR collapsed.) American policy makers saw the Soviet invasion of Afghanistan as an opportunity to deal their adversary a costly defeat, and to check the spread of Soviet-backed communism. The United States funneled military aid to the forces fighting the Soviet occupation.

Ultimately, Soviet forces were unable to put down the mujahideen. In 1988, after nearly a decade of brutal fighting, Soviet troops began pulling out of Afghanistan. The withdrawal was completed by February 1989.

Some participants in the conflict saw the outcome in religious terms: waging a jihad, or holy war, devout Muslims had defeated and humiliated one of the world's two superpowers. In 1988 a wealthy Saudi who'd financed and outfitted Arab fighters in Afghanistan formed a new group to wage jihad elsewhere. His name was Osama bin Laden, and his group was called al-Qaeda ("the Base").

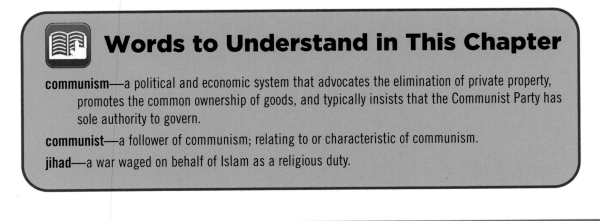

Words to Understand in This Chapter

communism—a political and economic system that advocates the elimination of private property, promotes the common ownership of goods, and typically insists that the Communist Party has sole authority to govern.

communist—a follower of communism; relating to or characteristic of communism.

jihad—a war waged on behalf of Islam as a religious duty.

Soviet troops in armored vehicles patrol a rural area of Afghanistan. The Soviet invasion in 1979 drew international condemnation. Soviet troops remained in the country for more than a decade.

Al-Qaeda and the Taliban

For a time, Bin Laden was considered a hero in his native land. But he had a falling-out with Saudi Arabia's monarchy. The trigger was Iraq's August 1990 invasion and occupation of its tiny but oil-rich neighbor, Kuwait.

Iraq and Kuwait both border Saudi Arabia to the north. Saudi leaders worried that Saddam Hussein, Iraq's dictator, had designs on their territory as well. Osama bin Laden offered to lead Arab units he'd organized during the Afghanistan conflict to repel a possible Iraqi invasion of Saudi Arabia. Instead, the Saudi monarchy allowed American forces to deploy in the country. In early 1991, under the auspices of the United Nations, the United States led an international military coalition that defeated Iraq and liberated Kuwait.

Any threat Saddam Hussein might have posed to Saudi Arabia had been eliminated, but Bin Laden was furious. In his

view, it was unacceptable that American infidels, or unbelievers, had been permitted in the land of the prophet Muhammad's birth. Bin Laden harshly criticized the Saudi monarchy, which eventually led to his banishment. He settled first in Sudan but was expelled from that country in 1996, after which he moved to Afghanistan. There, a group known as the Taliban had recently taken power.

The Taliban believed that modern influences had corrupted Afghan society and the way Islam was practiced. They sought to restore a supposedly pure form of Islam as it had existed (they believed) during the seventh century, in the time of the Prophet and the generations that immediately followed. To do this, the Taliban imposed an ultraconservative version of sharia, or Islamic law. So, for example, Afghans were forbidden to listen to music, watch television, or use the Internet. Girls weren't allowed to attend school past the age of eight. Women weren't

An Afghan mujahideen demonstrates how to use a hand-held surface-to-air missile—probably provided by the United States as part of a secret program to destabilize the Soviet Union by supporting the rebels. After the victory over the Soviets, some of the mujahideen set up the Taliban government.

Osama bin Laden had fought with the *mujahideen* in Afghanistan during the Soviet occupation. He wished to rid Muslim countries of Western influences.

permitted to hold jobs and, in fact, weren't even allowed to leave their home without their husband's or father's permission. When they did appear in public, females had to be accompanied by a male relative and covered from head to toe in a garment called a burqa. People who violated these and other aspects of the Taliban-imposed sharia were subject to draconian punishments, including execution.

Broadly, Osama bin Laden shared the Taliban's perspective on religious matters. He, too, held a highly conservative interpretation of Islam; he, too, believed Muslim societies had been corrupted by modern ideas and practices, particularly from the West. But whereas the Taliban's ambitions didn't extend beyond governing Afghanistan, Bin Laden wanted to replace regimes across the Arab world that he considered un-Islamic, especially the Saudi monarchy. Bin Laden and his al-Qaeda associates labeled these Arab governments "the near enemy." They could be defeated, in the analysis of al-Qaeda, by depriving them of support from foreign powers ("the far enemy").

Chief among the far enemy was the United States. Using terrorism as a tactic, al-Qaeda planned to compel the United States to disengage from the Middle East—just as another superpower, the Soviet Union, had previously been forced to withdraw from Afghanistan.

"They Are All Targets"

In February 1998, Osama bin Laden and four associates issued a statement that amounted to a declaration of war against the United States. Killing Americans, the statement said, was the "individual duty for every Muslim who can do it in any country in which it is possible to do it." A few months later, an American TV reporter interviewed Bin Laden in Afghanistan. Asked whether it was acceptable to attack civilians, he responded, "We do not have to differentiate between military or civilian. As far as we are concerned, they are all targets."

On August 7, 1998, al-Qaeda operatives detonated powerful truck bombs at the U.S. embassies in two East African countries, Kenya and Tanzania. Combined, the blasts killed 224 people, including 12 Americans. About 5,000 were wounded.

In response, President Bill Clinton ordered cruise-missile strikes against al-Qaeda targets. But because of poor intelligence and bad luck, the strikes were a failure. Bin Laden had left an al-Qaeda training camp in Afghanistan hours before cruise missiles rained down on it. A target in Sudan that the administration said was an al-Qaeda chemical-weapons factory turned out instead to be an ordinary pharmaceutical plant. Its destruction created an international outcry.

Another al-Qaeda attack occurred in October 2000. Two men piloted an explosives-laden skiff into the hull of an American warship, the USS Cole, at anchor in the port of Aden, Yemen. The attack claimed the lives of 17 American sailors.

At this point, however, most Americans knew little if anything about Osama bin Laden and al-Qaeda. That would all change on a crystal-clear morning in the late summer of 2001.

The "Planes Operation"

Sometime in 1996, a Kuwaiti named Khalid Sheikh Mohammed met with Osama bin Laden in Afghanistan. During the late 1980s, Mohammed had joined the mujahideen fighting against the Soviet occupation in Afghanistan. Before that, he'd obtained a degree in mechanical engineering from a university in North Carolina. Now, Mohammed pitched an ambitious terrorist plan to al-Qaeda's leader. It involved hijacking 10 passenger airplanes simultaneously and flying 9 of them into targets on both the East Coast and the West Coast of the United States. The final airlin-

Workers search through the debris at Ground Zero, the remains of the World Trade Center in New York City. The September 11 attacks were planned by a terrorist group that was being sheltered in Afghanistan.

er would be landed, and, after all the adult male passengers had been murdered, a hijacker would issue to the news media a list of grievances against the United States. Bin Laden rejected Mohammed's plan as too expensive to mount and too complex to have a reasonable chance of succeeding.

In early 1999, however, Bin Laden notified Khalid Sheikh Mohammed that al-Qaeda would finance a pared-down version of his terrorist proposal. Planning began in earnest for what al-Qaeda operatives referred to as the "planes operation."

The plot was carried out on the morning of September 11, 2001. Wielding small knives or box cutters, four teams of al-Qaeda terrorists took control of four jetliners shortly after they'd taken off from airports on the East Coast. At 8:46 a.m.,

one of the hijacked planes slammed into the North Tower of New York City's World Trade Center. Everyone on board the plane, and hundreds of people in the building, died instantly. An intense fire, fed by thousands of gallons of jet fuel and tons of flammable debris, trapped more than a thousand people above the 99th floor, the uppermost area of the impact.

At 9:03, another hijacked plane struck the South Tower of the World Trade Center between the 77th and 85th floors. As with the earlier impact, the crash killed hundreds of people immediately and trapped many others on the floors above the ensuing fire.

The high-temperature fires in the World Trade Center's twin towers undermined the buildings' structural integrity. Just before ten o'clock, the South Tower collapsed. A half hour later, the North Tower fell.

Aerial view of the destruction caused when a hijacked commercial airliner crashed into the Pentagon on September 11, 2001. All 62 people on board the aircraft were killed, along with 125 people in the Pentagon.

By that time, additional horrors had unfolded elsewhere. At 9:37 a third hijacked jetliner had crashed into the Pentagon, outside Washington, D.C. The Pentagon serves as the headquarters for the U.S. Department of Defense. Shortly after ten o'clock, a fourth hijacked plane crashed in a field in western Pennsylvania following a struggle between passengers and the terrorists. The intended target may have been the U.S. Capitol Building.

All told, the shocking attacks claimed nearly 3,000 lives. The effects on American government and policy—including immigration policy—would be profound.

 **Text-Dependent Questions**

1. Who were the *mujahideen?*
2. Name the founder of al-Qaeda.
3. Which targets did the hijacked planes hit on September 11, 2001?

Research Project

Interview a parent or someone else who is old enough to remember the terrorist attacks of September 11, 2001. What are the person's most vivid recollections of that day?

3 FOCUSING ON HOMELAND SECURITY

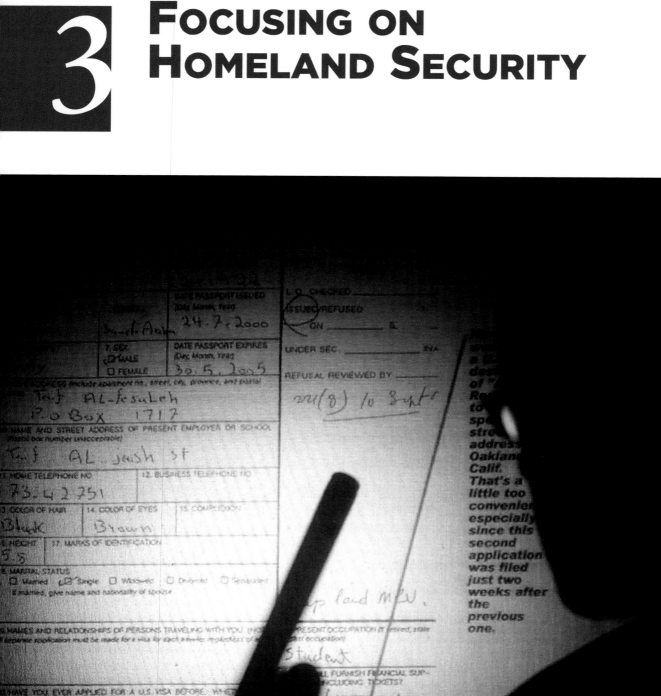

In the aftermath of the September 11 terrorist attacks, questions emerged as to why the U.S. government had failed to detect and stop the plot. After all, Bin Laden hadn't made a secret of his intention to "bring the fighting to America," as he said in two separate interviews. During the spring and summer of 2001, U.S. intelligence and law enforcement agencies had, in fact, uncovered multiple clues that a major al-Qaeda strike was coming. But the chances of preventing the attack were hampered by, among other factors, a lack of information sharing among the various agencies and decision makers responsible for national security and counterterrorism.

In an attempt to address that issue, and to close other vulnerabilities to terrorism, Congress passed the Homeland Security Act. President George W. Bush signed the act into law on November 25, 2002.

The Homeland Security Act mandated a major reorganization of the U.S. government. It created the Department of Homeland Security (DHS), a vast new cabinet department. More than 20 federal agencies and departments were brought under the authority of DHS.

◀A reporter points out an error in the visa application of Hani Hanjour, one of the terrorists involved in the attacks of September 11, 2001. Some deportable aliens enter the United States with fraudulent visas; others enter with legitimate documents but fail to meet the specific conditions of their visa while they are living in the country.

Immigration Reorganization

The September 11 attacks had exposed gaps in U.S. immigration enforcement. The 19 hijackers were all foreigners: they included an Egyptian, a Lebanese, two men from the United Arab Emirates, and 15 from Saudi Arabia. They'd all entered the United States legally, on tourist, business, or student visas. However, a significant portion were in the country illegally at the time of the attacks, as they'd overstayed their visas.

The Homeland Security Act abolished the Immigration and Naturalization Service (INS), a seven-decade-old agency that had operated under the Department of Justice, and brought its responsibilities under the purview of the Department of Homeland Security. A new agency, U.S. Citizenship and Immigration Services (USCIS), was established to oversee lawful immigration to the United States, the issuance of work authorization to foreign nationals, and related matters.

U.S. Customs and Border Protection (CBP), another new agency operating under DHS, would become the largest federal law enforcement agency. As of 2016, it had more than 60,000 employees. Its Customs and Immigration inspectors check the documents of travelers to the United States at air, sea, and land ports of entry, seeking to prevent terrorists and others without proper authorization from entering the country. CBP's inspectors also examine arriving cargo. CBP's Border Patrol agents monitor the U.S. borders with Mexico and Canada in order to prevent illegal immigration.

Words to Understand in This Chapter

infraction—a violation of a rule or law.

matriculate—to enroll as a student at a college or university.

port of entry—a place where a person may legally enter a country.

removal proceedings—the legal process by which the government seeks to deport a foreign national who isn't authorized to be in the country.

A protester declares her opposition to new rules requiring that men living in the United States who entered on temporary visas and were born in predominantly Muslim nations register with U.S. immigration authorities. Critics charged that the rules unfairly discriminated against residents of Middle Eastern origin.

Under the government reorganization brought about by the Homeland Security Act, the task of enforcing immigration and customs laws in the interior of the United States fell to U.S. Customs and Immigration Enforcement (ICE). ICE investigators attempt to identify and arrest undocumented immigrants, particularly those who might pose a threat to national security. ICE officers also oversee the deportation of illegal immigrants.

Controversial Policies

As far as immigration is concerned, the creation of the Department of Homeland Security was arguably the most consequential response to the September 11 attacks. But the government instituted a range of new policies and practices in the name of protecting the country. Some proved highly controversial. For example, the Justice Department implemented a "voluntary interview program" of Muslim and Arab male immi-

President George W. Bush, flanked by members of Congress, signs the Enhanced Border Security and Visa Entry Reform Act, May 14, 2002. The legislation, passed in response to the September 11, 2001, terrorist attacks on the United States, tightened rules on the granting of visas.

grants between the ages of 18 and 33—who, it was asserted, "fit the criteria of people who might have information regarding terrorism." Thousands were interviewed before the program was ended in late 2002.

In addition, in the months after the September 11 attacks, the government took into custody—often without arrest warrants—some 1,200 foreign nationals who were of Middle Eastern or South Asian descent and who were Muslim. Many were held for long periods without charge, and some were prevented from contacting a lawyer. The government even refused to release the detainees' names or disclose where they were being held. Secret evidence was used in immigration hearings closed to the public and the press.

Under a program called the National Security Entry-Exit Registration System (NSEERS), which was instituted in late 2002, visitors identified as presenting an elevated risk to national security—including anyone from Iran, Iraq, Libya, Sudan, or Syria—were required to register, be fingerprinted and photographed, and submit to a lengthy interview when they arrived at a U.S. port of entry. On the day they left the United States, affected travelers had to complete a departure registration at a designated port.

NSEERS had another component, known as "Special Registration." It affected males age 16 and older who'd come to the United States from certain countries and who weren't naturalized U.S. citizens or lawful permanent residents. These people had to report to a designated immigration office to register. There they were fingerprinted, photographed, and interrogated at length. Of the 25 countries of origin covered under the Special Registration program, 24 were Muslim-majority nations (North Korea was the lone exception).

Registration proceeded in four stages of about one to two months each, with members of specific nationalities ordered to report during a given stage. The first called in were from Iran, Iraq, Libya, Sudan, and Syria. Next came men from Afghanistan, Algeria, Bahrain, Eritrea, Lebanon, Morocco, North Korea, Oman, Qatar, Somalia, Tunisia, the United Arab Emirates, and Yemen. Stage 3 of Special Registration was reserved for Pakistanis and Saudis; stage 4, for Bangladeshis, Egyptians, Indonesians, Jordanians, and Kuwaitis.

Special Registration had its share of critics. The program, opponents charged, wasn't adequately publicized, and thus many men exposed themselves to penalties, including possible criminal charges, simply because they were unaware of the requirement that they report to an immigration office and register. Additionally, of the approximately 84,000 Arabs and Muslims who did comply with the program, around 14,000 were detained and placed in removal proceedings—in many cases, according to critics, for minor infractions or inadvertent oversights. And the program didn't lead to any terrorism charges, though Attorney General John Ashcroft claimed in 2003 that Special Registration had uncovered eight suspected terrorists. Critics were skeptical even of that very limited claim. Why, they wondered, would an actual terrorist report to an immigration office to register?

The Department of Homeland Security modified NSEERS in

December 2003, suspending a requirement that covered aliens re-register every year, and eliminating a follow-up interview that port-of-entry registrants were supposed to undergo after 30 to 40 days in the country. President Barack Obama finally terminated NSEERS completely in 2011.

Instead of singling out individuals based on their religious affiliation or nationality, the immigration screening measures in use today are more broadly applied. Since 2009, for example, almost every U.S. port of entry has been using a program called US-VISIT (U.S. Visitor and Immigration Status Indicator Technology), which DHS had begun phasing in six years earlier. US-VISIT collects fingerprints and photos of all noncitizens admitted into the United States, and the resulting records can be cross-checked against other government databases, including the Federal Bureau of Investigation's massive database of fingerprints.

Similarly, foreigners studying in the United States are tracked through the Student and Exchange Visitor Information System, or SEVIS. Schools report when foreign students matriculate, change majors, drop out, or graduate. SEVIS checks student biographical information against government criminal and terrorist databases.

Under most circumstances, a citizen of certain eligible countries may visit the United States for up to 90 days without obtaining a visa. As of 2016, some three dozen countries—mostly in Europe—were participants in the Visa Waiver Program. To take advantage of the program, foreign nationals must enter the United States from Mexico or Canada at an official land border crossing, or they must arrive on an approved airliner or cruise ship, in which case they must submit biographic information before their plane or ship departs for the United States. That information is collected by the Electronic System for Travel Authorization (ESTA). Launched in 2009, ESTA checks the traveler's data against terrorist watch lists and other U.S. government databases.

How effective are these sorts of measures? Is the country more secure today than it was before 2001? Do the millions of undocumented immigrants already in the United States constitute a serious national security risk? What about the tens of thousands, or hundreds of thousands, who arrive each year? Before attempting to answer these questions, it's useful to look at undocumented immigration more generally.

Text-Dependent Questions

1. Which country did most of the September 11 hijackers come from?
2. Which immigration agency did the Homeland Security Act abolish?
3. What does NSEERS stand for?

Research Project

Find out which countries participate in the Visa Waiver Program.

THOSE LIVING IN THE SHADOWS

ost undocumented immigrants seek to enter the United States knowing that—even if all goes well—they'll be living in the shadows of American society. They won't legally be able to get a job. They won't be allowed to vote. Other than emergency medical treatment, they'll be ineligible for all the benefits and entitlements American citizens and legal immigrants take for granted. And, in the not-unlikely event they're caught, they'll be subject to detention and deportation. Any money they've spent to get to the United States—which often amounts to thousands of dollars—will be lost. Given these realities, why do unauthorized migrants continue to come to the United States?

Obviously, there's no single answer to that question. Different undocumented immigrants have different motivations. Broadly, however, it's fair to say that among undocumented immigrants, the prospect of living in the United States seems better than the alternative of remaining in their own country. For some (such as the young Guatemalan profiled in chapter 1 of this book), that's because the home country is racked by high levels of violence—whether that means a full-fledged war, strife

◀A woman shakes hands after a job interview. All job applicants in the United States must present identification to prove their legal status. Since the passing of the Immigrant Reform and Control Act (IRCA) in 1986, employers have been held responsible for checking the official documents of job candidates.

between different ethnic or political groups, gang violence, or something else. People who live in constant fear for their safety, or for the safety of their loved ones, have a powerful reason to move somewhere else.

Many migrants take the risk of entering the United States illegally for the political and social freedoms the country offers. Americans enjoy freedom of speech, freedom of movement, and freedom of religion. These are the purest gifts the nation has to offer, and under some repressive regimes throughout the world, such freedoms are nonexistent.

Economic opportunity also draws many undocumented immigrants to the United States. That's the case even though undocumented immigrants—lacking legal authorization to work—tend to end up in employment situations most Americans would considerable undesirable (for example, in physically demanding and low-wage work, or doing off-the-books jobs in the "shadow economy," which leaves the immigrants vulnerable to employer exploitation). Despite all this, the jobs available to undocumented immigrants in the United States are often much higher paying than the jobs available in the poverty-stricken countries they left. Being relatively poor in the United States represents, for many undocumented immigrants, a higher standard of living than they were used to in their home country. Many undocumented immigrants send money home to family members who've remained in their native land. Collectively, these remittances amount to tens of billions of dollars annually.

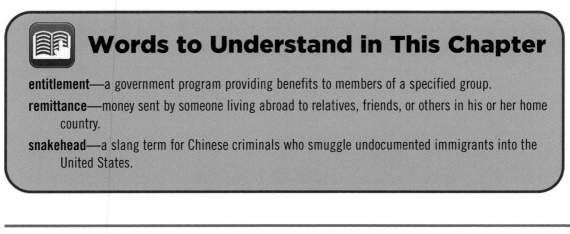

Words to Understand in This Chapter

entitlement—a government program providing benefits to members of a specified group.

remittance—money sent by someone living abroad to relatives, friends, or others in his or her home country.

snakehead—a slang term for Chinese criminals who smuggle undocumented immigrants into the United States.

Where Do Undocumented Immigrants Come From?

Crewmembers from the Coast Guard Cutter *Kathleen Moore* rescue Cubans migrants from an uninhabited island near the Bahamas, December 2015. The men were trying to sail their small boat to the United States, but it foundered.

As noted, Mexicans and Central Americans make up the majority of unauthorized immigrants in the United States—together, they accounted for more than two-thirds of the undocumented population in 2012, according to estimates by the Pew Research Center. In total numbers, Pew estimated that there were 5.85 million undocumented Mexicans, and 1.7 million undocumented Central Americans.

More than a million additional undocumented immigrants hailed from elsewhere in the Western Hemisphere. An estimated 700,000, or 6.3 percent of the total undocumented population, came from South America. The leading South American source countries were Colombia (with about 150,000 unauthorized immigrants), Ecuador (130,000), and Peru (120,000). Some 550,000 people from Caribbean nations were living illegally in the United States. That constituted nearly 5 percent of the total

undocumented population. The Dominican Republic, with approximately 150,000 individuals in the United States without authorization, was the top Caribbean source country. It was followed by Haiti (110,000) and Jamaica (100,000). An estimated 120,000 Canadians were also living in the United States illegally in 2012.

Asians account for a substantial proportion of the undocumented immigrants in the United States. Pew Research Center estimates for 2012 placed the figure at 12.4 percent. Of the estimated 1.4 million Asian unauthorized immigrants, 450,000 were from India, 300,000 from China, 200,000 from the Philippines, and 180,000 from Korea.

Nearly half a million people in the United States illegally in 2012 were from Europe. That amounted to about 4.3 percent of the total undocumented population.

Undocumented immigrants like this construction worker typically find jobs that do not require great scrutiny of their credentials. Other typical fields of employment for undocumented immigrants are farm labor, land-scaping, garment making, and domestic service.

Undocumented immigrants from the rest of the world, including Africa and the Middle East—arguably the region of greatest concern for the security of the U.S. "homeland"—totaled approximately 400,000. That represented 3.5 percent of the total undocumented population.

Getting In

Most unauthorized immigrants enter the country by bypassing inspection. In most cases, that means slipping across the U.S. land border with Mexico. Illegal crossings of the border with Canada are less frequent. Though it's by no means a precise measure, because the southern border is more heavily monitored and patrolled than the northern border, illegal-alien apprehensions at the borders offer a good overall picture. In fiscal year 2015 (October 2014–September 2015), more than 331,000 undocumented migrants were caught along the Mexico border. For the same period along the Canadian border, the figure was just 2,626.

For many would-be illegal immigrants who live outside continental North America, a land crossing isn't feasible. Such a crossing would first involve a trip to Mexico or Canada, potentially adding considerable expense, time, and uncertainty to the journey. Smugglers specializing in bringing undocumented immigrants to the United States from Asia have found a lucrative niche. In China, these smugglers are often referred to as "snakeheads." They typically squeeze undocumented Chinese aboard commercial ships, charging $50,000 or more per passenger for the trip across the Pacific Ocean. Undocumented immigrants from India and Pakistan are also smuggled to North America aboard freighters.

To avoid detection, smugglers often conceal undocumented immigrants inside cargo containers. In April 2016, for example, authorities stumbled onto one such smuggling operation when an illegal alien fell and broke his ankle while climbing out of a cargo container as freight was being off-loaded from a Chinese vessel, the Maple River, at the Port of Long Beach, California.

Twenty-two other undocumented immigrants were subsequently found packed inside two cargo containers. The 23 Chinese aliens had spent about three weeks in the containers, as the Maple River sailed from China to Vancouver, Canada, and on to Long Beach. "They were living in deplorable conditions," a Long Beach emergency responder said of the immigrants, who were treated at local hospitals before being turned over to Immigration and Customs Enforcement. "Fortunately, the top of the container was canvas and not steel, which provided better ventilation for them."

While some snakeheads pack their human cargo into steel containers measuring 20 feet (6 meters) or 40 feet (12.1 meters) long by 8 feet (2.4 meters) wide, other smugglers modify their ships. They build false walls around the inside of the ship's hull. Often the space between the false wall and the hull is so narrow that the illegal immigrants who are concealed there can't turn around or lift their arms.

Needless to say, a weeks-long journey cooped up in a small space, often in darkness and without sanitation, is highly unpleasant. But it can also be dangerous. Illegal immigrants sometimes suffocate inside cargo containers. Sometimes they die of dehydration or disease. If the ship they're aboard founders, drowning is a distinct possibility. That fate befell Chinese illegal immigrants in an infamous incident in 1993.

A snakehead gang had packed 286 Chinese illegal immigrants in the hot, dark hold of a freighter called the Golden Venture. The ship departed from Thailand and sailed west to Mombasa, Kenya. It then proceeded southward, sailing around the tip of Africa before setting a northeastward course for New York. On June 6, 1993, the Golden Venture hit a sandbar and became stuck a couple hundred yards off Rockaway Beach in Queens, New York. The snakeheads released the migrants from the ship's hold and encouraged them to swim for shore, telling them that if they set foot on the beach, they could apply for asylum in the United States. The distance wasn't far, but the water was cold, and the migrants were hungry and exhausted after

A father with his daughter on his shoulders marches with hundreds of thousands of immigrants in Los Angeles. A majority of illegal immigrants come from Mexico and Central America.

Illegal immigrants tend to settle in large cities like Los Angeles or New York, where they hope to blend in to the large populations and where work is available for people who don't have proper documentation.

having spent four months crammed into a space about the size of a two-car garage. Ten of them drowned. The survivors were picked up and detained by the INS.

Evading the Law

If the majority of undocumented immigrants get into the United States by avoiding ports of entry, a significant number initially arrive in the country with valid documents but stay past the legally authorized period. These "overstays" are estimated to account for 40 percent of the total undocumented population. However, because the government only began compiling and analyzing detailed data on overstays in fiscal year 2015, long-term trends among that group are, as of the publication of this book, impossible to discern.

According to the Department of Homeland Security, nearly 45 million foreign nationals arrived by air or sea with valid business or tourist visas during fiscal year 2015. Of that group, 482,781, or about 1.07 percent, remained in the United States past the expiration date of their visas. However, about 66,000 foreign nationals who'd overstayed left the country in the first three months of fiscal year 2016, according to the Department of Homeland Security.

In an attempt to get past immigration inspectors, some foreign nationals present fraudulent documents at U.S. ports of entry. These can be either custom-made forgeries with false information or genuine passports of someone other than the holder. Technological changes have made forgery more difficult, but forgers are always searching for new strategies.

While some fake documents are homemade, the most effective ones are official papers that have received some slight changes. U.S. passports can be stolen or purchased from Americans for $1,000 or more. Immigration inspectors have expert training in detecting fraudulent documents. However, the enormous volume of travelers to the United States means that even with a high detection rate, some people with false documents will inevitably be able to enter the country.

Where Do Undocumented Immigrants Settle?

In 2012, according to a study by the Pew Research Center, just half a dozen U.S. states were home to about 6 of every 10 foreign nationals in the country illegally. California had by far the largest undocumented population, with an estimated 2.45 million. It was followed by Texas (1.65 million), Florida (925,000), New York (750,000), New Jersey (525,000), and Illinois (475,000).

By contrast, six states had fewer than 5,000 undocumented immigrants each in 2012, according to the Pew study. They were Maine, Montana, North Dakota, South Dakota, Vermont, and West Virginia.

Pew found shifting settlement patterns among the undocumented. Seven states, it said, had seen growth in the numbers of unauthorized immigrants between 2009 and 2012. Those states were Florida, Idaho, Maryland, Nebraska, New Jersey, Pennsylvania, and Virginia. By contrast, the undocumented population decreased in 14 states: Alabama, Arizona, California, Colorado, Georgia, Illinois, Indiana, Kansas, Kentucky, Massachusetts, Nevada, New Mexico, New York, and Oregon. For the remaining 29 states, the number of undocumented immigrants remained stable between 2009 and 2012, according to the Pew study.

 Text-Dependent Questions

1. From which country do the largest number of undocumented immigrants in the United States come from?
2. What was the *Golden Venture*?
3. Which six U.S. states are home to the largest populations of undocumented immigrants?

Research Project

To become a U.S. citizen, an immigrant from another country must pass a civics test. U.S. Citizenship and Immigration Services offers practice tests at: https://my.uscis.gov/prep/test/civics/view
    Take a test. What percentage did you get correct? Do some further research about any answers you got wrong.

5 ENFORCEMENT ON THE BORDER AND IN THE COURTS

Even before the terrorist attacks of September 11, 2001, the United States had devoted considerable resources to stopping the flow of illegal immigrants. Most of the efforts were concentrated along the U.S.-Mexico border, the area included within the U.S. Border Patrol's Southwest Border Region. The Southwest Border Region is divided into nine sectors: San Diego and El Centro (California); Yuma and Tucson (Arizona); and Big Bend, El Paso, Laredo, Del Rio, and Rio Grande Valley (Texas).

Holding the Line

In September 1993, Border Patrol officers in the El Paso sector began Operation Hold the Line. Instead of trying to chase down undocumented immigrants who'd already crossed the border, Operation Hold the Line sought to deter those immigrants from crossing in the first place. The strategy involved stationing a host of Border Patrol agents in plain view along a 20-mile (32-km) stretch of border between Ciudad Juárez, Mexico, and El Paso, where an estimated 8,000 undocumented immigrants had been crossing every day. Since the region has flat terrain, the agents

◀ View of the border crossing station at Los Algodones, on the border between Mexcio and Arizona.

could be seen from (and could see for) a great distance. With an agent usually in sight, fewer people risked crossing. After the operation got under way, apprehensions fell by more than 70 percent.

Politicians in California soon began clamoring for a similar program to stop illegal immigration into San Diego from Tijuana, Mexico. President Bill Clinton obliged, in 1994, with Operation Gatekeeper. Hundreds of new Border Patrol agents were trained and deployed in San Diego, and the sector's budget was doubled.

But the deterrent strategy used in Operation Hold the Line wasn't transferable to San Diego because of topographic differences. Border Patrol agents in El Paso had excellent lines of sight because of the level terrain, and undocumented immigrants had to cross a natural barrier, the Rio Grande. No such natural barrier separates Tijuana from San Diego, and the area's hilly terrain impedes visibility. On the Mexican side of the border, steep ravines and heavy undergrowth offer would-be illegal immigrants many places to hide.

Operation Gatekeeper was launched in the fall of 1994 with a test project along a five-mile (8-km) stretch of border called Imperial Beach. The success of that undertaking convinced officials to expand the program throughout the 66 miles (106 km) of the sector, stretching eastward from San Diego to El Centro.

The first improvements were made to the hardware along the border. Multiple fences were erected. Whereas undocumented immigrants previously had to climb one fence, now they would have to climb three in many places. And they would have to do

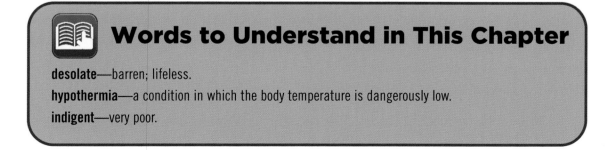

📖 Words to Understand in This Chapter

desolate—barren; lifeless.

hypothermia—a condition in which the body temperature is dangerously low.

indigent—very poor.

A well-lit fence divides the border between Tijuana, Mexico, and San Ysidro, California. The fence was one of the technical improvements that emerged from Operation Gatekeeper in 1994.

so quickly, since bright lights on the fences would keep them exposed until they'd completely climbed over the last fence.

New hardware on the border also obstructed attempts to tunnel under the fences. Deep steel plates were installed to stop tunnels at midpoint.

Border Patrol agents also were supplied with a variety of high-tech equipment. This included infrared scopes, for spotting illegal immigrants hidden in brush, and motion sensors.

In 1997, another major operation to secure more of the border began. Operation Rio Grande essentially extended Operation Hold the Line into two additional sectors. It included the hiring of additional Border Patrol agents to staff those sectors, as well as the construction of new roads, to allow the agents to respond more quickly when undocumented immigrants were detected near the border. As with Operation Gatekeeper, a vari-

An officer with U.S. Immigration and Customs Enforcement (ICE) searches an illegal immigrant in Florida.

ety of high-tech equipment was also deployed in Operation Rio Grande.

In one respect, the new border-enforcement operations were successful: they dramatically reduced illegal immigration in the sectors in which they were implemented. Nonetheless, the undocumented population continued to grow steadily, because the border-enforcement operations merely shifted where aliens crossed into the United States. Instead of entering the country at cities like El Paso and San Diego or their suburbs, illegal immigrants began crossing in remote, rugged areas like the Sonoran Desert in Arizona. When people try to walk through this inhospitable region, deaths from dehydration, heatstroke, and hypothermia are inevitable.

From 1994 to 2015, the remains of some 7,000 presumed border-crossers were found in the desolate borderlands of the southwestern United States, mostly in Arizona. But that, according to experts, represents only a portion of the actual death toll. Many bodies, they say, are never discovered.

Since the late 1990s, some immigrant advocates have been calling for the United States to abandon, for humanitarian reasons, the "enforcement through deterrence" border strategy that began with Operation Hold the Line. By channeling undocumented migrants away from easy-to-cross border spots and into remote and dangerous areas, critics say, the strategy results in needless suffering and death. But supporters of strong border enforcement are generally unmoved by that argument, insisting that those who decide to enter the United States illegally are ultimately responsible for any harm that might befall them.

A New Legal Tool

In addition to stepped-up border enforcement, the 1990s witnessed a key change in U.S. immigration law that allowed for the speedy deportation of certain undocumented immigrants. The measure, known as "expedited removal," was included in the Illegal Immigration Reform and Immigrant Responsibility Act of 1996.

Previously, if a foreign national denied entry into the United States for lack of valid documents refused to leave the country voluntarily, that person could only be removed by an immigration judge. This was expensive for the government and created a large backlog in immigration courts.

Expedited removal allows Customs and Border Protection officials to deport, often within a matter of hours and without a hearing before a judge, noncitizens lacking proper documents and seeking admission to the United States at a port of entry.

Undocumented immigrants apprehended within 100 miles (161 km) of the border with Mexico or Canada are also subject to expedited removal, unless they can demonstrate that they've been in the United States continuously for at least 14 days. However, DHS policy generally dictates that undocumented Mexicans and Canadians caught within 100 miles of the border be placed in proceedings before an immigration judge rather than going through expedited removal.

Undocumented immigrants who make an asylum claim also aren't subject to expedited removal. Rather, they're placed in detention pending a hearing of their asylum claim.

Aliens who do receive an order of expedited removal are barred for entering the United States again for at least five years. When the order of expedited removal has been issued because of fraud or misrepresentation, a lifetime ban on entry into the United States is imposed.

With the exception of expedited removal, the process of deporting an undocumented immigrant from the United States is typically drawn out. It can take months or even years.

Contact with the Authorities

Persons in the United States illegally may come to the attention of immigration authorities in a variety of ways. For instance, Immigration and Customs Enforcement officers might raid a workplace and discover undocumented workers there. An unauthorized immigrant might simply be waiting for a bus or train, or walking on the streets of a city or town within 100 miles of the border. In that zone, ICE and Border Patrol officers are permitted to ask anyone about his or her citizenship, conduct a warrantless search of the person's effects, and take the person into custody for questioning based only on the suspicion that he or she might be undocumented. An undocumented immigrant elsewhere in the country might be stopped by local police for a minor traffic violation, or arrested for a crime. If the police suspect the person is in the country illegally, they'll contact ICE. And sometimes it's ICE that contacts the local police, based on

ICE officers escort a Mexican man who is being deported. During 2015, ICE removed or returned 235,413 individuals. Of this total, 165,935 were apprehended while, or shortly after, attempting to illegally enter the United States. The remaining 69,478 were apprehended in the interior of the United States. Most of them were convicted criminals who fell within ICE's civil immigration enforcement priorities.

booking records that are posted on databases accessible to federal immigration authorities. In such instances, ICE will file a "detainer," which requires that the police hold the suspected illegal alien for up to 48 hours so that an ICE officer can be sent to question the person about his or her immigration status.

Once an undocumented immigrant has been discovered and arrested, an ICE deportation officer must decide whether to put the person in removal proceedings and, if so, what the charge or charges will be. Usually, the charge is unlawful entry into the United States, overstaying a visa, or a criminal arrest or previous conviction. All immigration-related charges are presented in a

document known as a Notice to Appear (NTA).

Some undocumented immigrants opt not to fight to remain in the United States, but instead accept an arrangement known as voluntary departure. It's available only to those who don't face criminal charges (deportation is an administrative matter). Voluntary departure can be particularly appealing to unauthorized immigrants being held in an ICE detention center, potentially for an extended period, who believe they are unlikely to prevail in immigration court. (Immigration courts are special courts that conduct removal, or deportation, proceedings. They operate under the auspices of the Executive Office for Immigration Review, or EOIR, an agency within the U.S. Justice Department.)

In voluntary departure, the alien gives up the right to apply for relief in immigration court and agrees to leave the country, at

ICE officials often track down those who have committed crimes in other countries but have been admitted to the United States. Such people are generally deported.

his or her own expense, after a brief grace period. During that time, the alien has the opportunity to settle his or her affairs in the United States.

Voluntary departure offers an important benefit: it doesn't place a removal order on the undocumented immigrant's record, which would bar the person from entering the United States again for a period of 5 or 10 years. Someone who has accepted voluntary departure may legally return to the United States (subject to certain limitations) after obtaining a green card.

Detain or Release?

Immigrants who wish to contest their removal from the United States have the right to present their case in immigration court. Because some immigration courts have large backlogs, aliens may wait many months for their cases to be heard. During that time, most are released from ICE custody under one of several arrangements. Some aliens are fitted with an electronic ankle bracelet that allows authorities to monitor their whereabouts at all times. Others deemed to present very little flight risk—for example, because they have young children, a steady job, and deep ties to the community—may be released on their own recognizance. Still others are released after posting a bond, ranging from $1,500 to more than $20,000, depending on how serious a flight risk they're considered.

Certain aliens, such as those suspected of having ties to major drug-smuggling gangs or to terrorism, are held without bond. This isn't at all controversial. Nearly everyone would agree that it's a necessary and prudent approach to keeping the nation safe.

However, many undocumented immigrants who don't seem to present much danger, including some asylum seekers, also languish in detention centers for long periods as they await the disposition of their case. Often, this is because the alien is unable to raise enough money to post the required bond.

In 2013, Syracuse University's Transactional Records Access Clearinghouse (TRAC) compiled and published ICE custody data for November–December 2012. For the 66,305 aliens released during that period, the average length of time spent in ICE custody was 31 days. But the range was very wide. Some 40 percent were released within three days of their arrest; that group included 9 of every 10 aliens who agreed to return voluntarily to their country of origin. At the other end of the range, one alien was released after seven years in detention. For those released on bond, the average detention time was 42 days. Nearly 3 percent of the detainees released had spent more than six months in custody.

Critics argue that ICE keeps too many immigrants in detention for too long. Except for truly dangerous aliens, they insist, detention is unnecessarily harsh. It's also expensive, costing American taxpayers about $160 per detainee per day—which comes to about $2 billion annually.

But others, including some members of Congress, defend high levels of detention for undocumented immigrants in removal proceedings. Such people, they say, need to be monitored carefully, and incarceration is the surest way of doing that.

Deportation Proceedings

In addition to detailing specific charges, a Notice to Appear instructs the alien to appear before an immigration judge on a specific date for a "master calendar" hearing. If the alien ignores the NTA and fails to appear for the hearing, the judge may issue an order of deportation.

In many respects, immigration proceedings resemble criminal cases. The undocumented immigrant has certain rights and protections, including the right to be represented by legal counsel. But whereas a public defender must be assigned to any criminal defendant who is too poor to hire his or her own lawyer, the government isn't obligated to provide counsel to indigent immigrants in removal proceedings. Aliens are responsible for finding their own legal counsel or, alternatively, representing themselves. Many immigrant attorneys represent poor clients pro bono (for free), however.

A master calendar hearing is a brief preliminary procedure

These detainees at a holding center in Brownsville, Texas, have illegally entered the United States through Mexico and are waiting to be processed. Similar detention centers are located in Puerto Rico and in many states. As of 2016, there are 57 detention centers.

that resembles the arraignment of a criminal defendant. The immigrant (generally through his or her lawyer) essentially answers the charges, disputing that the government's information is correct, or acknowledging that it is correct but claiming some grounds for relief. Depending on the circumstances, several forms of relief might be possible. The alien might claim a fear of persecution if returned to his or her home country, for example, and thus request asylum. An undocumented immigrant who has been in the country continuously for at least 10 years, and who hasn't gotten into serious trouble with the law, might be eligible for a form of relief known as cancellation of removal. An "exceptional hardship waiver" might be granted to an undocumented immigrant if the immigrant could show that his or her removal would create extreme hardship for a parent, spouse, or child who is an American citizen.

Such claims aren't adjudicated at a master calendar hearing,

which lasts just a few minutes. If the judge decides an immigrant's claims might conceivably be justified, he or she schedules an individual, or merit, hearing for a later date and quickly moves on to the next master calendar hearing.

The merit hearing unfolds like a criminal trial. A lawyer for the government—usually with ICE—essentially acts as a prosecutor, arguing the case that the alien should be deported. The immigrant's attorney (or the immigrant, if no counsel has been obtained) presents the case for relief. Evidence is introduced, and witnesses testify under oath and are cross-examined.

A merit hearing may last several days. At the conclusion, the immigration judge issues a ruling (there are no juries in immigration court), either granting the alien relief from deportation or issuing a deportation order.

The private quarters (opposite) and exercise area (above) of a typical detention facility. Many deportable aliens receive bail to avoid detention; however, the suspects of the investigation following the September 2001 attacks faced extended detention periods while their cases were resolved.

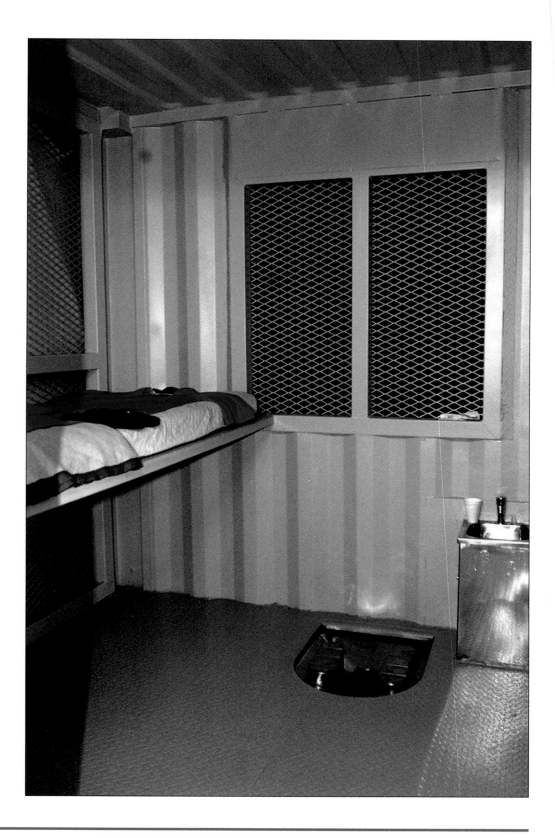

The Appeals Process

A deportation order issued by an immigration judge may be appealed. There are basically three types of appeals.

The first, and simplest, type of appeal is a called a motion to reopen, which is filed with the immigration court. It's appropriate if the alien uncovers facts or evidence relevant to the case but not available at the time of the merit hearing. A motion to reopen based on new facts or evidence must be filed within 90 days of the deportation order. A motion to open may also succeed if conditions in the alien's home country have changed since the hearing in such a way as to now put the alien at risk if deported. This situation might lead to the granting of asylum. A motion to reopen doesn't automatically stay (suspend) the deportation order while the court considers the appeal. The alien must request that the immigration court or immigration official issue a stay.

The second type of appeal is known as a motion to reconsider. It, too, is filed with the immigration court. A motion to reconsider asserts that the immigration judge who heard the alien's case made a mistake, either by misapplying the relevant law or by coming to an incorrect conclusion based on the facts and evidence. The motion to reconsider must detail, in very specific terms, how the judge erred. It must be filed within 30 days of the deportation order, and it doesn't automatically stay that order.

The third type of appeal goes through the Board of Immigration Appeals (BIA), an administrative body within the Justice Department's EOIR. The BIA, headquartered in Virginia, has jurisdiction to review the rulings of immigration courts nationwide. Most important for undocumented immigrants, it can uphold or overturn removal orders. It can also send a case back to the original immigration judge for reconsideration. On rare occasions, it may forward a case to the attorney general.

Appeals to the BIA must be made within 30 days of a deportation order. If an undocumented immigrant issued such an order appeals to the BIA within that period and without first filing a motion to reopen or a motion to reconsider with the immigration court, then the deportation order is automatically stayed pending a BIA decision.

BIA decisions are subject to judicial review by the U.S. Court of Appeals. In theory, a case could even reach the United States Supreme Court. But such an outcome would be highly unlikely.

 **Text-Dependent Questions**

1. Which Mexican city is across the Rio Grande from El Paso, Texas?

2. Why might an undocumented immigrant opt for voluntary departure rather than trying to contest his or her deportation in immigration court?

3. What's the difference between a motion to reopen and a motion to reconsider?

 **Research Project**

What is it like to be held at an Immigration and Customs Enforcement detention center? See if you can find a first-hand account.

6 THE THREAT: ACUTE, OR OVERBLOWN?

Much has changed since al-Qaeda terrorists brought down the twin towers of the World Trade Center. Most significantly, perhaps, the United States launched two major wars in the name of combating terrorism. The first, which began in October 2001, overthrew the Taliban government of Afghanistan and scattered al-Qaeda's leadership. The terrorist organization, though arguably weakened, wasn't eliminated. It became decentralized, with al-Qaeda "affiliates" arising in various countries across the Middle East and parts of Africa. Such groups publicly swore allegiance to al-Qaeda and subscribed to its jihadist philosophy, but they acted independently. Osama bin Laden, the longtime head of al-Qaeda, was killed in a 2011 U.S. Navy SEAL raid on his secret compound in Abbottabad, Pakistan. But Bin Laden had long since ceased exerting operational control over al-Qaeda.

The second major war launched in response to the September 11 terrorist attacks targeted Iraq. The administration of President George W. Bush insisted that the war, which began in March 2003, would be brief. That turned out to be tragically wrong. Similarly, the case the Bush administration had presented for justifying the war—that Iraq had links to al-Qaeda, had

◀ Protesters ask the government to deport illegal aliens, rather than granting them amnesty and allowing them to continue living in the United States.

chemical and biological weapons that it might share with terrorists, and was actively trying to develop nuclear weapons—turned out to be unfounded.

The U.S. invasion quickly plunged Iraq into chaos. Terrorists associated with al-Qaeda flocked to Iraq, fighting the U.S. occupation and helping to ignite a brutal civil war. The violence and disorder in Iraq, many analysts suggest, increased instability across the broader Middle East.

Elements of al-Qaeda in Iraq formed a group calling itself the Islamic State of Iraq and Syria (ISIS) in 2013. ISIS—which is also known as IS, ISIL, or Daesh—took advantage of chaos in Iraq and Syria to seize large swaths of territory in those countries. It set up a self-styled caliphate, or Islamic state, in that territory.

The United States gave military aid to allies fighting ISIS, including Kurdish forces in Iraq. Thousands of U.S. airstrikes also targeted ISIS.

For its part, ISIS called on devout Muslims across the globe to travel to Iraq and Syria to help defend the caliphate. ISIS urged those who were unable to undertake that journey, and who lived in the United States or other western societies, to wage jihad at home.

It's indisputable that extremist Islamic groups such as al-Qaeda and ISIS continue to wish harm on the United States. The vast majority of Muslims reject the radical philosophy and terrorist tactics of these groups. But, as the 2001 attacks demonstrated, even a relatively small number of terrorists can cause great carnage under the right circumstances.

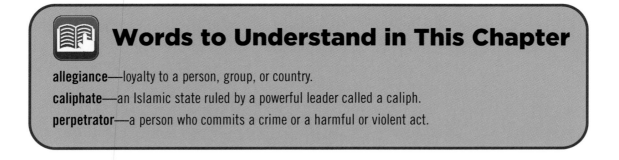

📖 Words to Understand in This Chapter

allegiance—loyalty to a person, group, or country.

caliphate—an Islamic state ruled by a powerful leader called a caliph.

perpetrator—a person who commits a crime or a harmful or violent act.

Thousands of people, many of them immigrants, participated in a march for immigration reform in Los Angeles.

Vast Expenditures

The United States has devoted vast resources to preventing terrorism. Between 2002 and 2016, the government spent more than $800 billion on homeland security.

Many observers believe securing the country's borders and deporting undocumented immigrants are vital to protecting the country. The annual budgets of U.S. Customs and Border Protection and U.S. Immigration and Customs Enforcement alone total about $20 billion. Along the northern border, the number of Border Patrol agents increased 500 percent from 2001 to 2015. There was no aerial coverage of the border with Canada in 2001. By 2015, drone aircraft monitored about 1,150 miles (1,851 km) of the northern border. In 2001, about 9,100 Border Patrol agents were assigned to the border with Mexico. In 2015, that number stood at more than 17,700. In addition,

the southern border contained about 650 miles (1,046 km) of fencing.

Despite all these efforts, some critics insist that U.S. border security remains inadequate, making the country more vulnerable to terrorism. "It is an acknowledged fact," wrote James A. Lyons, a retired admiral and former commander of the U.S. Pacific Fleet, in 2013, "that since we have refused to secure our borders, we have facilitated the transit and infiltration of al Qaeda affiliated terrorists . . . who are now living illegally in the United States. This is a serious national security issue." Not everyone would agree, however.

Illegal immigration and homeland security became a major political issue during the 2016 U.S. presidential campaign. The Republican nominee, businessman Donald Trump, called for the building of a wall along the entire length of the U.S.-Mexico border. He claimed such a wall—which would cost tens of billions

During the 2016 presidential election campaign, Republican Donald Trump (above) promised to build a wall between the United States and Mexico to prevent immigrants from crossing the border. Trump may not have been aware that such a wall already exists— the photo on the opposite page shows a section of the border wall in Arizona.

Part of an improvised memorial to victims of the Boston Marathon bombing in 2013. The bombers were immigrants who were living in the United States legally.

of dollars to construct—was necessary to address a growing wave of undocumented immigrants, among whom might be terrorists. "Just look at the record number of people right now that are pouring across the borders of this country," Trump remarked in April 2016.

Whatever else might be said about undocumented immigration, the assertion that it had reached record levels wasn't borne out by the facts. Studies consistently showed declining rates of illegal immigration, and those studies were supported by trends in border apprehensions. In 2005, according U.S. Customs and Border Protection, more than 1.7 million undocumented immigrants were caught along the southern border. In 2015, the number was just 331,333. Clearly, fewer people were trying to cross the border without authorization.

The overall undocumented population also declined. According to the Pew Research Center, the number of people living in the United States without authorization peaked in 2007 at an estimated 12.2 million, falling to an estimated 11.3 million by 2009 and essentially remaining level for the next five years. The decline was mostly attributable to the fact that more undocumented Mexicans returned to Mexico than arrived in the United States from Mexico.

Assessing the Risks

How significant a risk does undocumented immigration pose for the security of the U.S. homeland today? Should the government, in order to protect the nation from terrorism, devote even more resources to securing borders and deporting unauthorized immigrants?

These are difficult questions to answer. On the one hand, it's impossible to guarantee that foreign terrorists won't exploit vulnerabilities in U.S. immigration enforcement—either by slipping across a border or by arriving with valid visas and overstaying—and then go on to perpetrate another mass-casualty attack similar to the ones carried out by al-Qaeda on September 11, 2001.

On the other hand, as the 15th anniversary of the September

11 attacks approached, nothing remotely similar had taken place. Indeed, from September 12, 2001, through April 2016, a total of 45 people had lost their lives in the United States as a result of terrorism inspired by, or believed to have been inspired by, Islamic extremism. The majority of the deaths came from a handful of incidents:

- In November 2009, Nidal Hasan—a psychiatrist and major in the U.S. Army—went on a shooting rampage at the army base in Fort Hood, Texas. Hasan killed 13 people.
- In April 2013, two brothers, Tamerlan and Dzhokhar Tsarnaev, detonated a pair of homemade bombs near the finish line of the Boston marathon, killing three people. They later shot a police officer to death.
- Mohammad Youssef Abdulazeez attacked two military recruitment centers in Chattanooga, Tennessee, in July 2015. He killed four marines and a sailor.
- In December 2015, a married couple, Syed Rizwan Farook and Tashfeen Malik, went on a shooting spree at the Inland Regional Center in San Bernardino, California. They killed 14 people.

In none of these cases were the perpetrators in the United States illegally. Hasan was a U.S. citizen by birth. So was Farook, whose wife, Malik, had come to the United States legally on a fiancée visa. Abdulazeez, who was born in Kuwait, was a naturalized U.S. citizen. The Tsarnaev brothers were lawful permanent residents of the United States. In other words, none of the attacks would have been prevented by a tightening of border security or stepped-up deportation of unauthorized immigrants.

A U.S. Customs and Border protection station located in Fort Hancock, Texas. CBP is part of the United States Department of Homeland Security.

 **Text-Dependent Questions**

1. What is ISIS?
2. In what year did the undocumented population in the United States peak?
3. What terrorist incident were the Tsarnaev brothers responsible for?

 **Research Project**

Compile a timeline that details the rise of ISIS.

Chronology

c. 1000	Vikings land at L'Anse aux Meadows, Newfoundland; archaeological evidence suggests that a temporary settlement was established there.
1492	Christopher Columbus makes landfall in the Bahamas; his voyage opens the great era of European exploration and colonization in the New World.
1565	The Spanish establish St. Augustine; it is the oldest continuously inhabited European settlement in North America.
1607	Jamestown, Virginia, is established as the first permanent English settlement in North America.
1619	The first African-American slaves arrive in Virginia.
1620	Pilgrims seeking religious freedom land in Massachusetts and establish the Plymouth colony.
1775–83	The American Revolution is fought; immigration comes to a virtual standstill.
1796	Introduction of the Land Purchase Act; under the act, immigrants could buy 320 acres at $2 an acre.
1815	End of the Napoleonic Wars in Europe; beginning of European migration to America on a massive scale.
1861–65	Immigration to the United States comes to a virtual halt during the American Civil War, a bloody conflict between the Northern and Southern states.
1862	Adoption of the Homestead Act, which granted 160 acres of public land to a settler after a five-year occupancy; the Act helped settle the West.

1864   To address labor shortages during the Civil War, the Immigration Act of 1864 was passed to encourage immigration. The law also created a commissioner of immigration, appointed by the president to serve under the secretary of state.

1875   The first restrictive immigration statute, known as the Page Law, prohibited the immigration of criminals and Asians.

1882   Adoption of the Chinese Exclusion Act, which prevented Chinese laborers from immigrating for a ten-year period and resulted in the deportation of many unauthorized workers. The 1892 Geary Act extended this law for an additional ten years and required that Chinese nationals obtain identification papers.

1886   Installation and dedication of the Statue of Liberty, a gift from France, in New York Harbor.

1891	The Immigration Act of this year expanded the list of exclusions for immigration from prior laws to include those who have a contagious disease and polygamists. It also established a Bureau of Immigration as part of the federal government.
1892	Establishment of Ellis Island immigration station; by the time it closes in 1954, more than 12 million immigrants will be processed at the station.
1921	Congress passes the Emergency Quota Act; this law imposes numerical limits on immigrants for the first time.
1924	The National Origins Act becomes America's first permanent immigration policy, imposing further limits on immigration along with national quotas.
1939–45	World War II; thousands of Jews, among other Europeans, flee the war and are allowed entry to America as refugees.
1962	The Migration and Refugee Assistance Act was passed to help Cuban refugees fleeing the communist regime that had taken over the country.
1965	The Immigration and Nationality Act abolishes the quota system based on national origin; the new system still imposes numerical limits, but has many exemptions.
1980	The Refugee Act sets a limit on the number of refugees who will be admitted to the United States in a particular year.
1986	The Immigration Reform and Control Act makes it illegal for employers to hire immigrants who have not entered the country legally.
1990	The Immigration Act increases the number of legal immigrants permitted to enter the United States each year; Ellis Island is re-opened as a museum.
1996	Illegal Immigration Reform and Immigrant Responsibility Act sets easier standards for deportation.

2001	The Child Citizenship Act, which gives citizenship to children born outside of the United States who have at least one citizen parent, goes into effect in February.
2003	The Immigration and Naturalization Service (INS) is dissolved; a new agency in the new Department of Homeland Security, Citizenship and Immigration Services, takes over most INS functions.
2005	The REAL ID Act permits the federal government to construct barriers at national borders. The law also places more restrictions on immigrants.
2008	Activists protest against the construction of a security fence along the U.S. border with Mexico.
2012	President Barack Obama unveils Deferred Action for Childhood Arrivals (DACA), a program in which young adults (ages 15 to 30) brought to the U.S. illegally as children can apply for temporary deportation relief and a two-year work permit.
2014	President Obama expands DACA and adds a program that allows unauthorized immigrants who have lived in the U.S. at least five years and who have children that are U.S. citizens or legal permanent residents to apply for deportation relief and a three-year work permit. However, this program has not yet been implemented due to legal challenges.
2016	The population of the United States is estimated to be 323 million. The population of Canada is estimated at 36 million.

Series Glossary of Key Terms

assimilate—to adopt the ways of another culture; to fully become part of a different country or society.

census—an official count of a country's population.

deport—to forcibly remove someone from a country, usually back to his or her native land.

green card—a document that denotes lawful permanent resident status in the United States.

migrant laborer—an agricultural worker who travels from region to region, taking on short-term jobs.

naturalization—the act of granting a foreign-born person citizenship.

passport—a paper or book that identifies the holder as the citizen of a country; usually required for traveling to or through other foreign lands.

undocumented immigrant—a person who enters a country without official authorization; sometimes referred to as an "illegal immigrant."

visa—official authorization that permits arrival at a port of entry but does not guarantee admission into the United States.

Further Reading

Annerino, John. *Dead in Their Tracks: Crossing America's Desert Borderlands in the New Era*. Tucson: University of Arizona Press, 2009.

Bourke, Dale Hanson. *Immigration: Tough Questions, Direct Answers*. Downers Grove, IL: InterVarsity Press, 2014.

Broyles, Bill, and Mark Haynes. *Desert Duty: On the Line with the U.S. Border Patrol*. Austin: University of Texas Press, 2010.

Chebel d'Appollonia, Ariane. *Frontiers of Fear: Immigration and Security in Europe and the United States*. Ithaca, N.Y.: Cornell University Press, 2012.

Chomsky, Aviva. *Undocumented: How Immigration Became Illegal*. Boston: Beacon Press, 2014.

Gjelten, Tom. *A Nation of Nations: A Great American Immigration Story*. New York: Simon and Schuster, 2015.

Merino, Noel. *Illegal Immigration*. San Diego: Greenhaven Press, 2015.

Internet Resources

www.uscis.gov

The website of U.S. Citizenship and Immigration Services explains the various functions of the organization and provides specific information on immigration policy.

www.canadianhistory.ca/iv/main.html

This site contains an excellent history of immigration to Canada from the 1800s to the present.

www.cbp.gov

The homepage of U.S. Customs and Border Protection (CBP), an agency of the Department of Homeland Security, includes information about CBP's responsibilities, news, travel guidelines, and more.

www.ice.gov

This site is an informative source covering the operations of U.S. Immigration and Customs Enforcement, part of the Department of Homeland Security.

www.dhs.gov

The official site of the Department of Homeland Security offers an overview of the department's duties, news, press releases, and more.

http://www.aila.org

The homepage of the American Immigration Lawyers Association is a resource for advocates of fair immigration policy and for immigrants in need of legal counsel.

Index

Numbers in **bold italic** refer to captions.

Immigration and Refugee Protection Act (Canada), 31
Immigration Law and Procedure in a Nutshell (Weissbrodt), 73
Immigration Reform and Control Act (1986), 26, 65, 79
India, 39
interdiction, 33
internment camps, *47*

Johnson, Jason, *79*
Johnson, Lyndon B., *25*

al-Khalifa, Meriam, *79*
Korea, 39

Latin America, 37–39
Laughlin, Harry N., 23
Lennon, John, 50–51

Maali, Jesse, *52*
    See also subversives
marriage fraud, 47, 66
Metropolitan Detention Center, 84
    See also detainees
Mexico, 19, 24, 32, *38*, *41*, 42, 57, 60, *62*, 63, 75
Miami, Fla., *59*, 74, 77
migrant deaths, 58, *61*, 62–63
    See also aliens

Nazi Party, 47–49
New Jersey, 45
New Mexico, *55*
New Orleans, La., *59*
New York, 44, *69*
Nixon, Richard, 50–51
North Carolina, 45

Office of Legal Counsel (OLC), 86
Office of the Inspector General (OIG), 86
Operation Gatekeeper, 56–58
Operation Hold the Line, 56
Operation Rio Grande, 56
Operation Safeguard, *58*
    See also Border Patrol
Order to Show Cause, 70–71
    See also deportation

Passaic County Jail, 84
    See also detainees
Pearson, Lester, 30

See also Canada
Peru, 39
Philippines, 39
points system, 30–31
    See also Canada
population
    alien (undocumented immigrant), 28, 35–36, 38, 44–45
ports of entry, 19, 31–32, 33, 55
    See also aliens
Post-Order Custody Review (POCR), 86
prisons, 69
Puerto Rico, 69

al-Qaeda, 83
    See also terrorism
quotas, 23–26, 30
    See also ethnicity

Refugee Act of 1980, 26
    See also refugees
refugees, 24, 26, 29, 30–31, 78
"registry" provisions, 79
    See also discretionary relief
removal hearings, 47, 71–73, 77
    appeals, 80–81
        See also deportation
Reno, Janet, 74
Rio Grande, 55, 57, 61
San Diego, Calif., 56–58
San Ysidro, Calif., *57*
Scully, C. D., 23
September 11, 2001. *See* terrorism
Sinclair, John, 50
smuggling, 39–41, 61–63
"snakeheads," 40
    See also smuggling
Special Registration, 87
    See also terrorism
Student and Exchange Visitor Information System (SEVIS), 88
    See also visas
subversives, 51–53
    See also deportation

Temporary Quota Act of 1921, 23
    See also quotas
terrorism, *19*, 26, 27–29, *52*, 53, 70, 71–72, *73*, 83–88
Texas, 44, *55*, *58*
Thompson, Larry D., 87
Tijuana, Mexico, *57*

Contributors

Senior consulting editor STUART ANDERSON is an adjunct scholar at the Cato Institute and executive director of the National Foundation for American Policy. From August 2001 to January 2003, he served as executive associate commissioner for Policy and Planning and Counselor to the Commissioner at the Immigration and Naturalization Service. He spent four and a half years on Capitol Hill on the Senate Immigration Subcommittee, first for Senator Spencer Abraham and then as Staff Director of the subcommittee for Senator Sam Brownback. Prior to that, Stuart was Director of Trade and Immigration Studies at the Cato Institute, where he produced reports on the military contributions of immigrants and the role of immigrants in high technology. Stuart has published articles in the Wall Street Journal, New York Times, Los Angeles Times, and other publications. He has an M.A. from Georgetown University and a B.A. in Political Science from Drew University. His articles have appeared in such publications as the *Wall Street Journal*, *New York Times*, and *Los Angeles Times*.

MARIAN L. SMITH served as the senior historian of the U.S. Immigration and Naturalization Service (INS) from 1988 to 2003, and is currently the immigration and naturalization historian within the Department of Homeland Security in Washington, D.C. She studies, publishes, and speaks on the history of the immigration agency and is active in the management of official 20th-century immigration records.

PETER HAMMERSCHMIDT is director general of national cyber security at Public Safety Canada. He previously served as First Secretary (Financial and Military Affairs) for the Permanent Mission of Canada to the United Nations. Before taking this position, he was a ministerial speechwriter and policy specialist for the Department of National Defence in Ottawa. Prior to joining the public service, he served as the Publications Director for the Canadian Institute of Strategic Studies in Toronto. He has a B.A. (Honours) in Political Studies from Queen's University, and an MScEcon in Strategic Studies from the University of Wales, Aberystwyth.

RICK SCHMERHORN is a freelance writer and editor. A graduate of the University of Tennessee, he currently lives in New York City with his wife and children. This is his first book.

Picture Credits